ARCHAEOLOGY FOR KIDS

AUSTRALIA

TOP ARCHAEOLOGICAL DIG SITES AND DISCOVERIES
GUIDE ON ARCHAEOLOGICAL ARTIFACTS
5TH GRADE SOCIAL STUDIES

Speedy Publishing LLC

40 E. Main St. #1156

Newark, DE 19711

www.speedypublishing.com

Copyright 2017

All Rights reserved. No part of this book may be reproduced or used in any way or form or by any means whether electronic or mechanical, this means that you cannot record or photocopy any material ideas or tips that are provided in this book

In this book, we're going to talk about the top archaeological dig sites in Australia. So, let's get right to it!

There are many fascinating dig sites in Australia where fossil animals, plants, and stone artifacts from human civilizations have been found. It's believed that the first humans settled in Australia about 50,000 years ago.

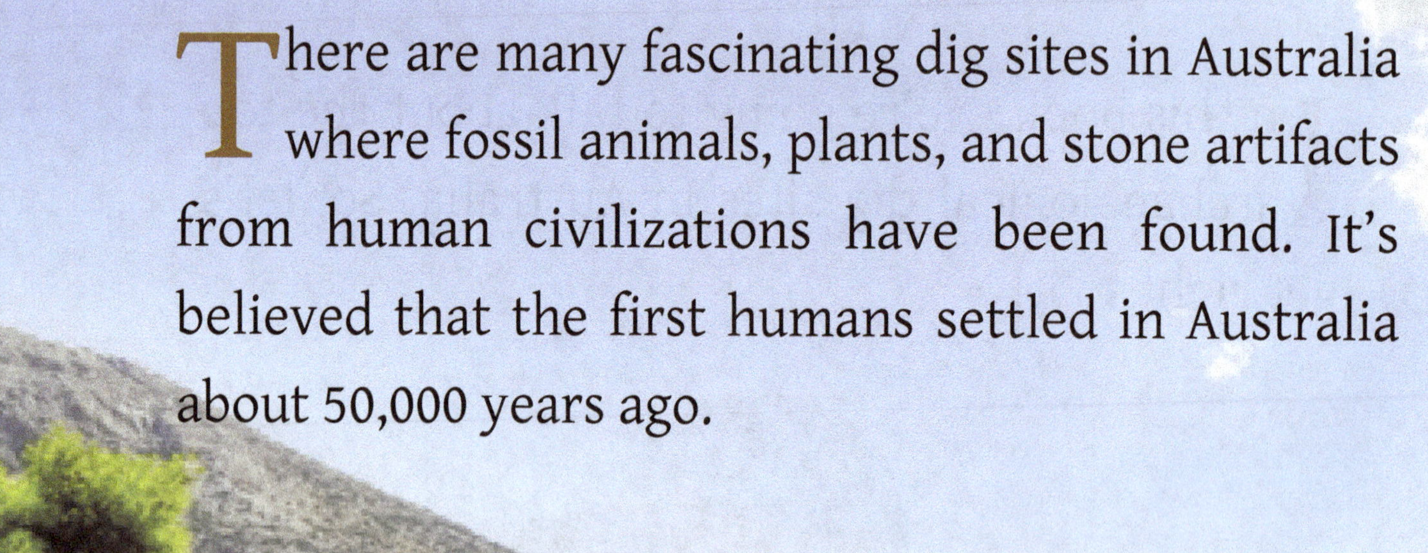

THE HISTORICAL SITE OF
MYCENAE, IN GREECE

CUDDIE SPRINGS

Cuddie Springs is a shallow lake in New South Wales near the city of Carinda. This amazing fossil site has bones belonging to megafauna. The word "megafauna" just means very large animals.

Archaeologists have found remains of many different animals there, such as:

- Diprotodon, the largest marsupial that ever lived, similar to a modern-day wombat

• Sthenurus, an extinct type of kangaroo
STHENURUS

- Genyornis, a huge flightless bird that was much taller than a man
- Macropus titan, an extinct vertebrate belonging to the kangaroo family
- Large wombats
- Giant reptiles

LARGE WOMBAT

The fossil finds date back to about 30,000 years ago. In addition to the animal bones there are also artifacts with traces of blood and hair. The stone implements found were all used for processing animal carcasses, not for hunting and killing these giant animals.

DINOSAUR FOSSIL

Archaeologists believe that once the animals were stuck in the mud and died, the humans carved them up for food.

It's also possible they were hunted elsewhere and brought to the site for cooking. There were hearths for fire cooking found at the site.

Grindstones for the processing of plants, such as grass seeds and acacia seeds, were found at this site as well. These artifacts are the oldest evidence that ancient Aboriginal people ground up plants 30,000 years ago. These grindstones are much older than those found in other locations in the world, about 20,000 years older.

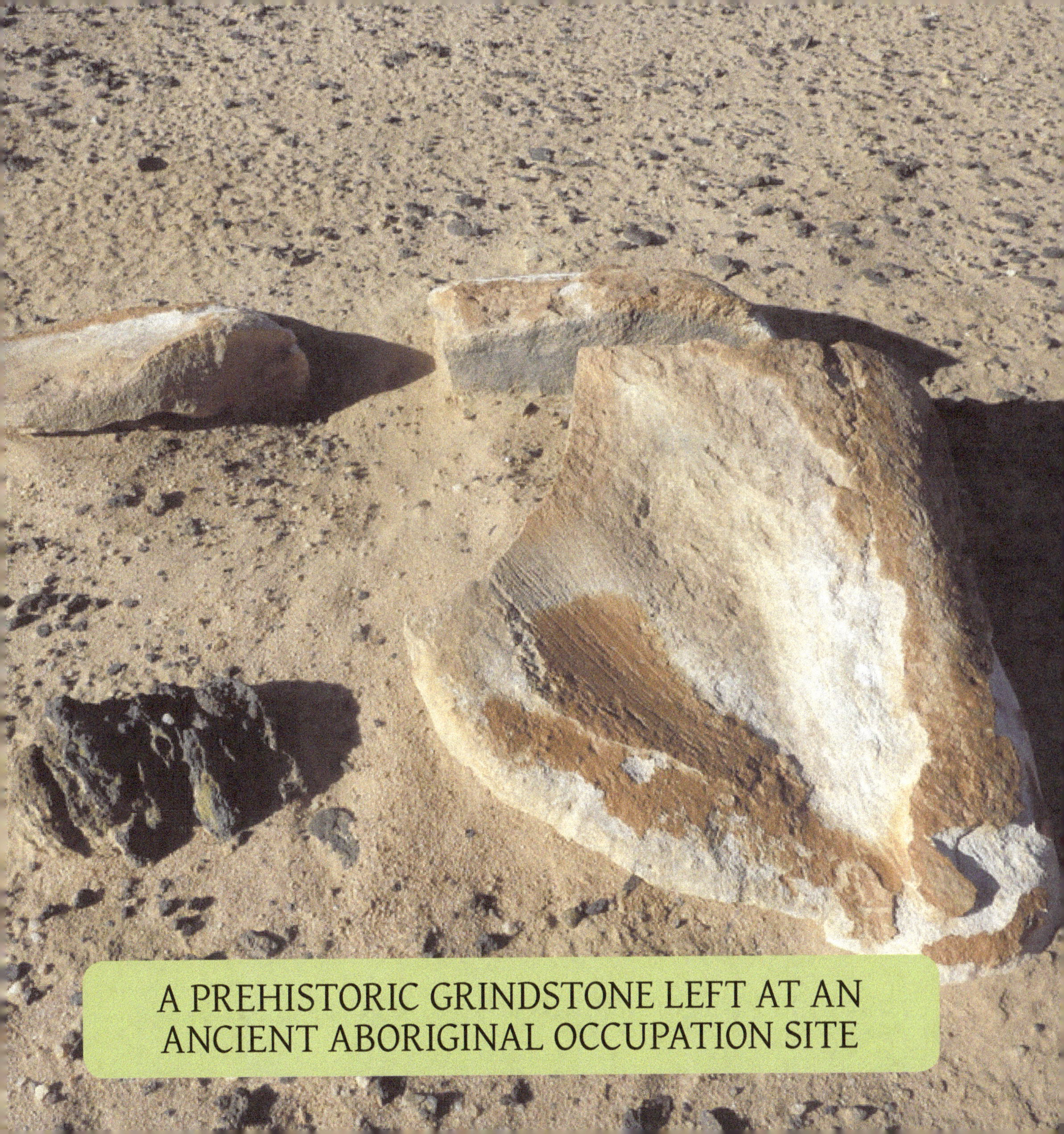

A PREHISTORIC GRINDSTONE LEFT AT AN
ANCIENT ABORIGINAL OCCUPATION SITE

One of the most important artifacts found at the site is a cyclon, which is a cylindrical stone that is weathered. One end of the stone had been ground down into the shape of a cone.

Archaeologists believe this type of stone was used for sacred rituals. When it was dated to the Pleistocene age, it was a surprising find since it shows that Aboriginal religious rituals had remained the same over thousands of years.

MURUJUGA NATIONAL PARK

MURUJUGA OR BURRUP PENINSULA

Murujaga, which is also called Burrup Peninsula, is located in the Dampier Archipelago in the western section of Australia. Amazing ancient petroglyphs can be found on the rocks in this area. It's estimated that there are half a million to a million of these designs carved there

It is the largest find of this kind anywhere in the world and the largest archaeological site of indigenous or native Australian culture. In addition to its scientific significance, it also has huge spiritual significance to the aboriginal people living today since the people who created these carvings were their ancient ancestors.

Some of the petroglyphs are small engravings such as Emu tracks. Others are large drawings of aboriginal ceremonies, such as figures climbing up the mast of a ship. There are many interesting animals depicted such as Tasmanian tigers, which are now extinct, sea turtles, whales, kangaroos, and emus.

They also include the world's oldest known image of a human face. In addition, there are a large number of megaliths, which are arrangements of large stones, similar to Stonehenge in England.

Archaeologists estimate that the petroglyphs there may be 30,000 or 40,000 years old. Unfortunately, it's not possible for archaeologists to date these engravings precisely. That's because there was no color pigment used on these images.

Cave paintings have organic residue from the pigments that were used to create them so they can be dated. Also, open-air rocks don't have layers such as fossils in underground caves. The rocks in the area have been tested using special cosmic radiation testing and they are 40,000 Bc or older, but that doesn't give a precise indication of when the engravings were made.

RED OCHER PIGMENT

Occasionally, clumps of red ocher pigment have been found, but it isn't clear whether these were used to create art or whether they were used for face or body paint, a widespread aboriginal tradition. This site is in danger of being destroyed by industrial development and it's not clear why action hasn't been taken to protect this important site.

SUNBURY EARTH RINGS

The Sunbury Earth Rings near the city of Sunbury, Victoria were first studied in the early 1970s. These prehistoric "rings" were created by ancient aboriginal people. They scraped off areas of grass as well as topsoil.

SUNBURY VICTORIA AERIAL

Then, they piled these materials in a ridge that was circular in shape. The rings are different sizes. Some are only 10 meters in diameter while others are as wide as 25 meters, but all are on gently sloping hills. Dr. David Frankel did the first excavation and he found two cairns. A cairn is a pile of stones that was created by human hands.

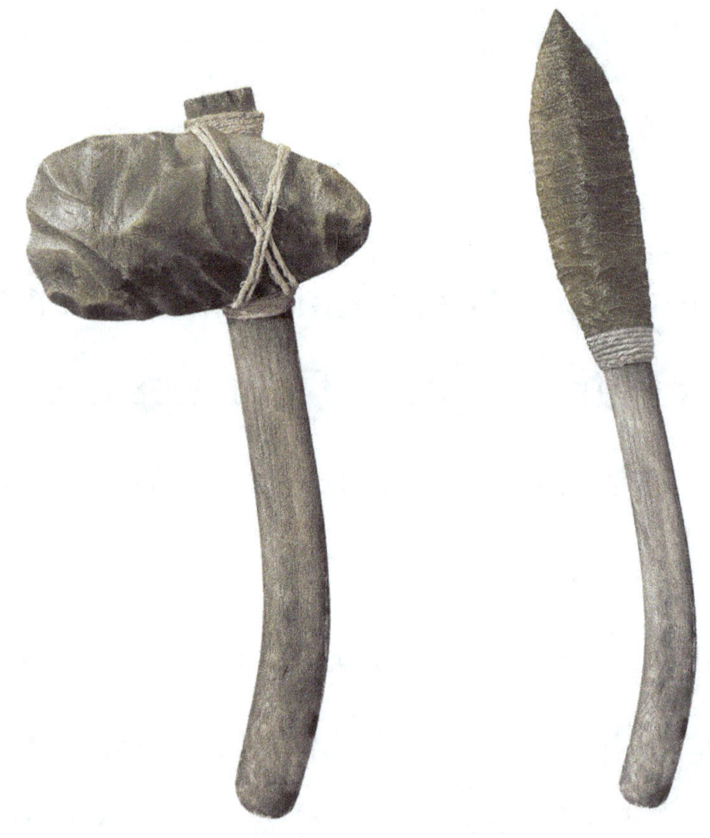

He also discovered some sharp knives made of stone. Archaeologists believe that the rings could have been the location of ancient

ceremonies where the indigenous peoples created scars on their bodies. The site may be at least 1,000 years old.

KOW SWAMP ARCHAEOLOGICAL SITE

Kow Swamp is located in northern Victoria. The skeletons of 40 prehistoric people have been found there. It's the largest burial site worldwide that dates back to the late Pleistocene and contains a single population. The burials took place sometime between 13,000 to 9,500 years BP, which means before the present time period. The skeletons are of men and women and also juveniles and infants. It's a very important prehistoric site.

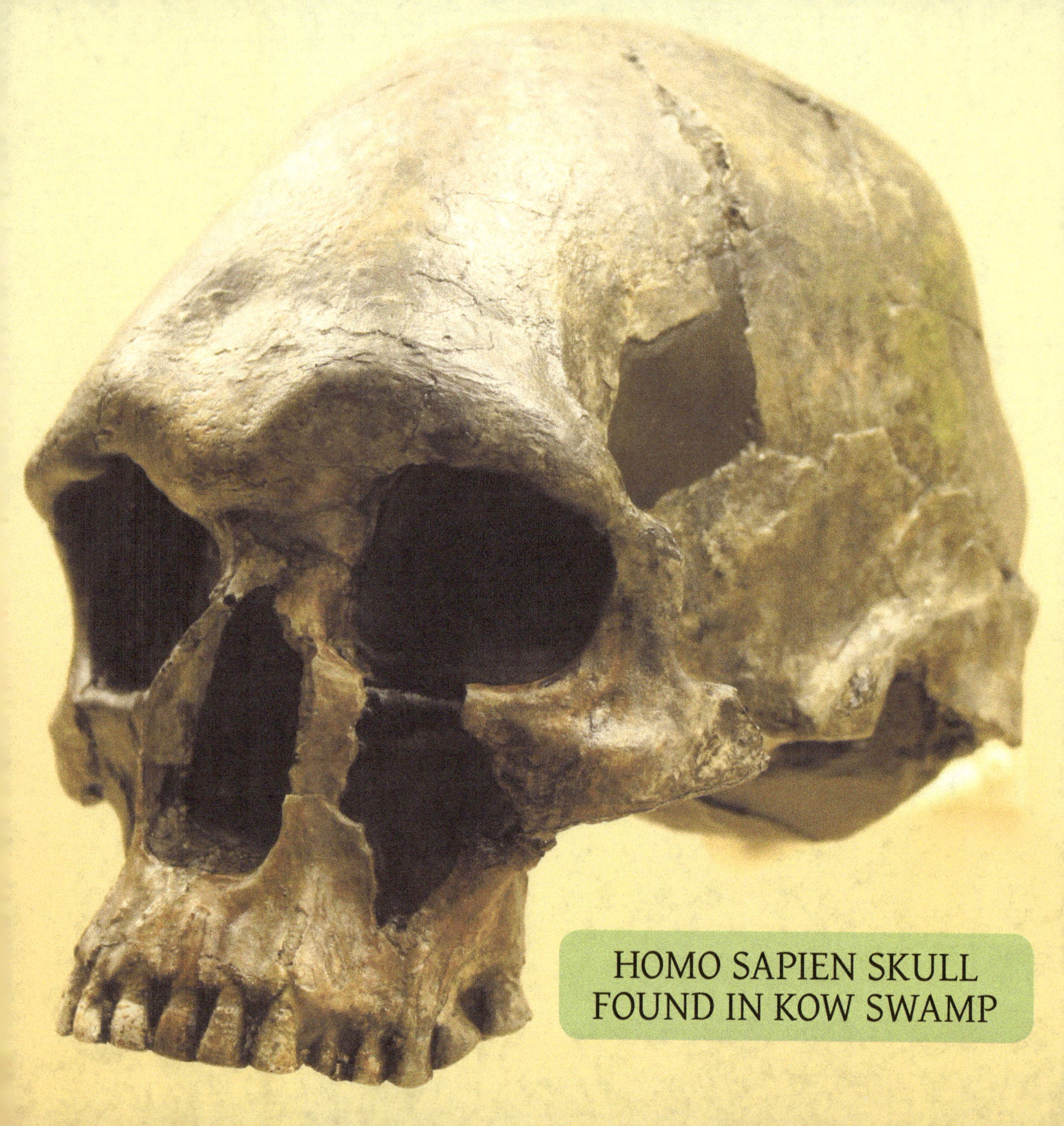
HOMO SAPIEN SKULL
FOUND IN KOW SWAMP

The skeletons had long heads that were quite large and they had bones that were very thick. They had very prominent ridges for their eyebrows and foreheads that receded. They also had massive jaws with very large teeth, some of which were even larger than the teeth of Java Man. The teeth were very ground down. Archaeologists believe that these people used grindstones to crush seeds. When they ate the seeds there was quite a bit of pulverized stone mixed with them, which would cause their teeth to be ground down over time.

There were goods buried in the graves with the bodies as well, such as shells from mussels, artifacts made from stone, teeth from marsupial animals, and ocher, which is a natural reddish pigment.

SEASHELL FOSSIL

EXCAVATED CAVE IN
WESTERN AUSTRALIA

DEVIL'S LAIR

Devil's Lair is a large limestone cave with just one chamber. It's located in Western Australia and is believed to be one of the first sites where human beings lived on the continent. Charles Dortch was the first archaeologist to excavate there in the 1970s. Although there have only been a few artifacts found there, they give profound insights into these ancient people.

S ome of the artifacts discovered are beads made
of bone and a stone piece that is perforated
and is thought to be a pendant. These items are
important because they show some of the earliest

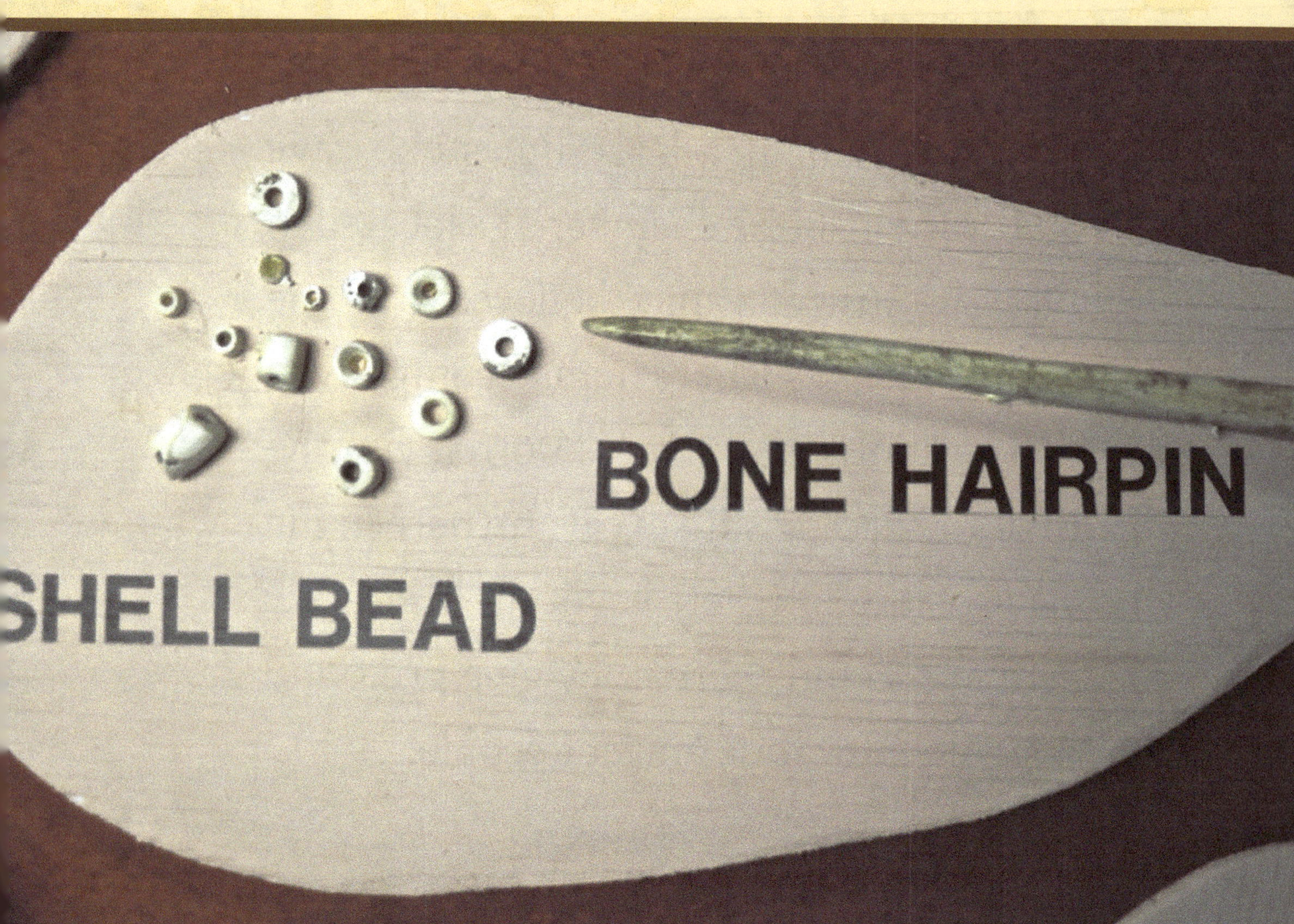

BONE HAIRPIN
SHELL BEAD

types of human behavior using symbols. Four hearths, one nested inside the other, have been found there, which date back over 40,000 years.

WILLANDRA LAKES
NATIONAL PARK

LAKE MUNGO

Lake Mungo is located in the Willandra Lakes region, which is New South Wales. In 1969, geologist Jim Bowler discovered skeletal remains, which were later called the Mungo Lady and Mungo Man. They are thought to be the most important such remains ever discovered in Australia.

Dated to 42,000 years ago, they are some of the earliest remains of Homo sapiens or modern humans that have been found outside the African continent.

They show evidence of the spiritual beliefs of early humans since the bodies were cremated.

THE NANYA FAMILY

These ancient remains are important to the Aboriginal people who still live in this area. In addition to these ancient human remains, there are also remains of waste from the preparation of food, evidence of hearths and fireplaces, and the wastes from the creation of stone tools. Points, sharp knives, axes, and grindstones for the cutting of meat and plants have all been found.

There's also an abundant amount of waste flakes from a process called knapping. Knapping is striking a stone piece usually flint, chert, or obsidian to make a tool out of stone.

BIRD MOTIF KNAPPING SET

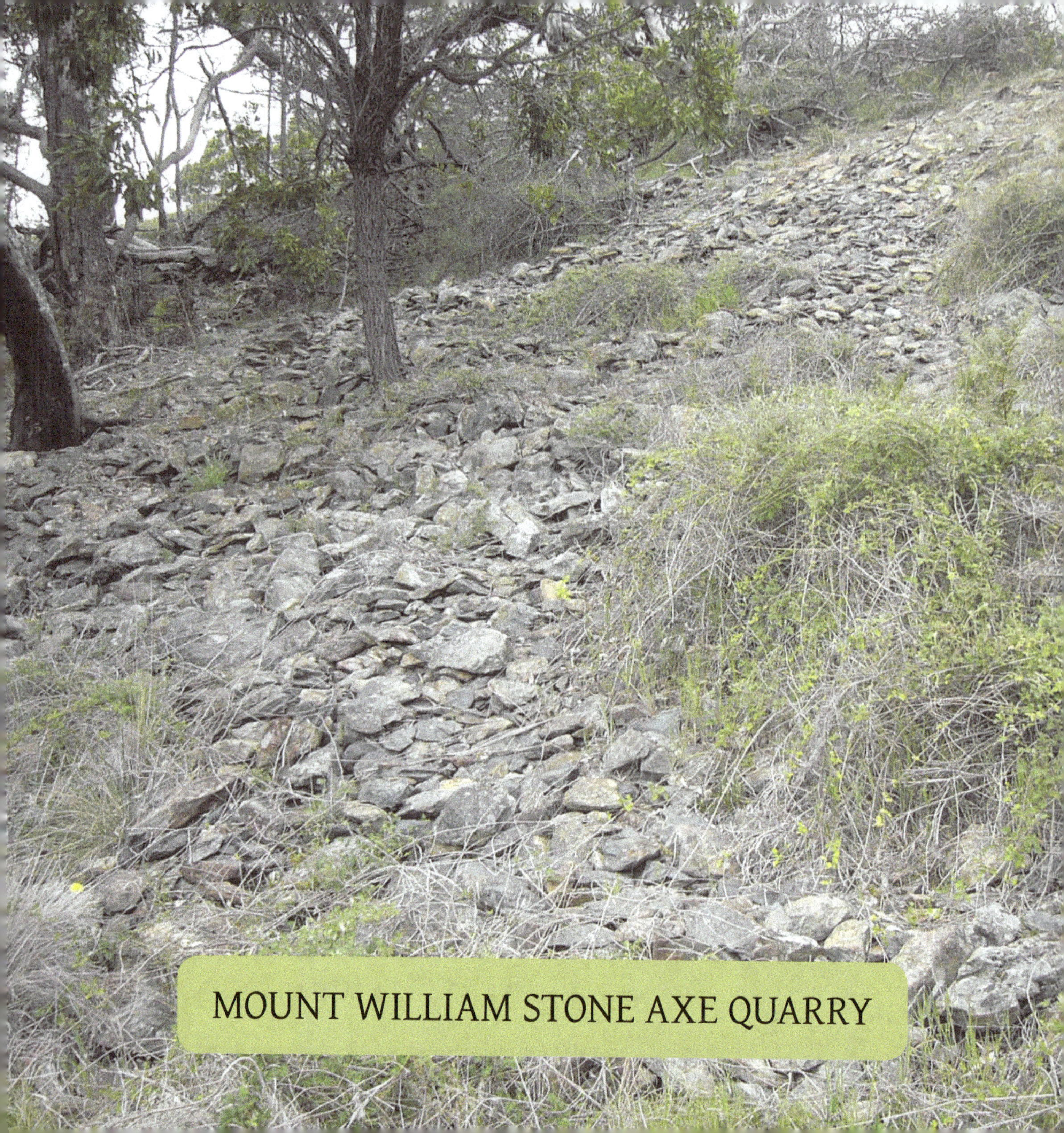

MOUNT WILLIAM STONE AXE QUARRY

MOUNT WILLIAM STONE AXE QUARRY

Mount William in Central Victoria is the site of an ancient stone quarry. As wooded areas began to expand 1500 years ago, the Wurundjeri people started to adapt to their new environment. They began to quarry greenstone at this location to create hatchet heads for trading as well as hunting.

A stone hatchet became a critical must-have tool in every Aboriginal camp. The stone pieces were attached to handles made of wood and were used for many different purposes, such

as shaping wood to make shields or spears, cutting holes in trees to capture opossums, or to split open tree trunks to get honey or insect grubs to eat.

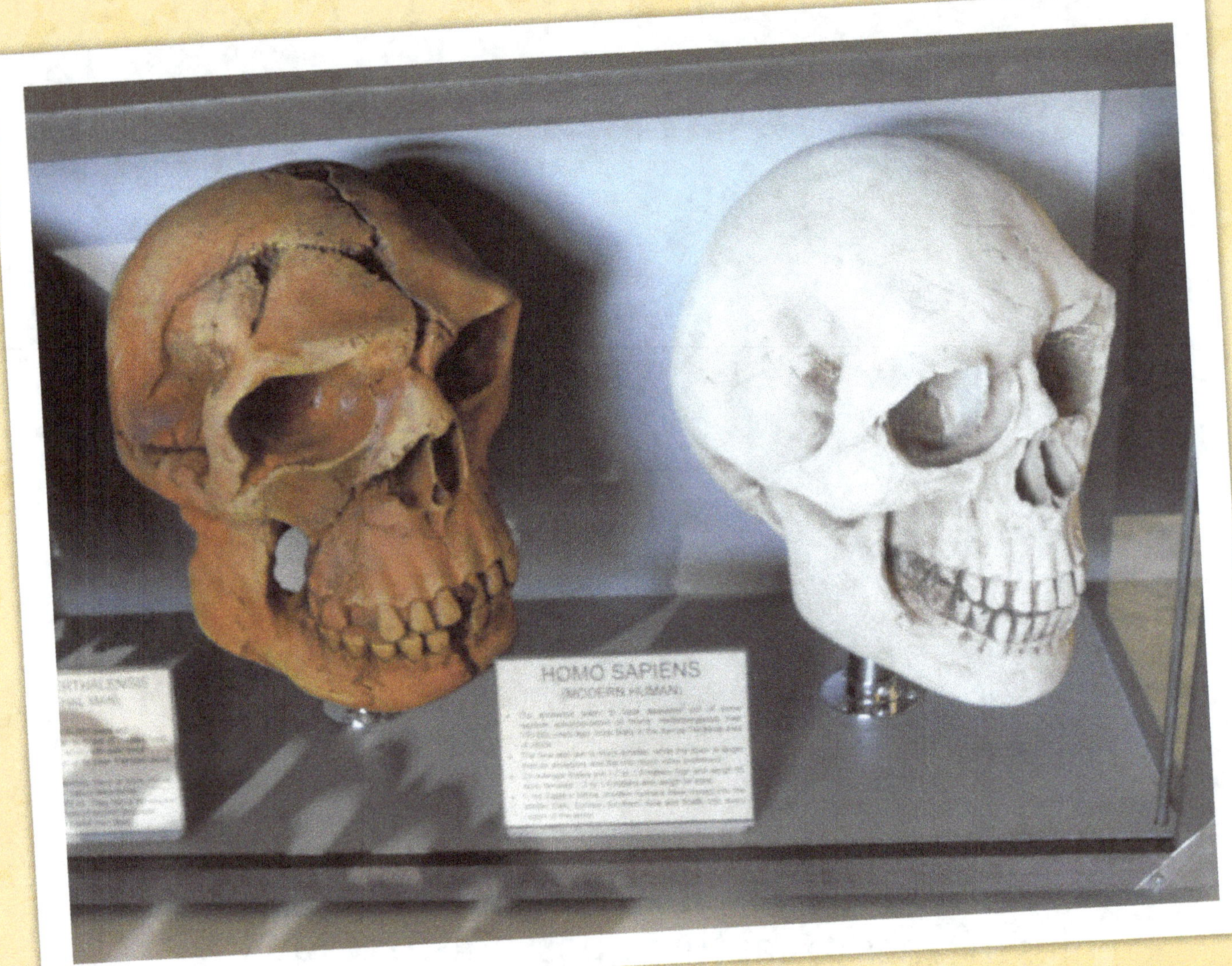

HOMO SAPIENS' SKULL

SUMMARY

There's evidence that Homo sapiens settled in Australia as early as 50,000 years ago. Archaeological digs give clues to the tools these humans used, the animals that they lived with and ate, and the sacred ceremonies they practiced.

Awesome! Now that you've read about some of the amazing archaeological finds in Australia you may want to read about Australia in the Baby Professor book Australia and Oceania: The Smallest Continent, Unique Animal Life – Geography for Kids | Children's Explore the World Books.

Visit
BABY PROFESSOR
EDUCATION KIDS
www.BabyProfessorBooks.com
to download Free Baby Professor eBooks
and view our catalog of new and exciting
Children's Books

www.ingramcontent.com/pod-product-compliance
Lightning Source LLC
Chambersburg PA
CBHW080542110726
47973CB00005B/61